P9-AQY-076

A gift for

In appreciation for what God has done through you!

From

Date

Lifting Up the Teacher's Heart

Scriptures, Prayers, and Poems of Encouragement
for every season

Jane Wilke

www.CTAinc.com
Lifting Up the Teacher's Heart
*Scriptures, Prayers, and Poems of Encouragement
for every season*

Scripture quotations are taken from the HOLY BIBLE, NEW INTERNATIONAL VERSION®. Copyright © 1973, 1978, 1984 International Bible Society. All rights reserved throughout the world. Used by permission of International Bible Society.

The poem on pages 43–44 is from Mountain Breezes by Amy Carmichael. Copyright © 1999 The Dohnavur Fellowship. Published by CLC Publications, Fort Washington, PA. Used by permission.

Copyright © 2004 by CTA, Inc., 1625 Larkin Williams Rd., Fenton, MO 63026-1205.

ISBN 0-9754499-2-3
Printed in Thailand

CONTENTS

*The LORD will watch over your coming
and going both now and forevermore.*

PSALM 121:8

LIFTING THE
EYES OF
YOUR HEART

When I stepped out in faith and allowed you to lead, Lord, you provided more than I hoped for.

AUTHOR UNKNOWN

God's fingers can touch nothing but to mold it into loveliness.

GEORGE MACDONALD

O Lord, you are our Father. We are the clay, you are the potter; we are all the work of your hand.

ISAIAH 64:8

Dear One Who Leads My People,

May the eyes of your heart be enlightened so that you may know the depth of my love for you and be assured of the living hope that is yours through the death and resurrection of my Son.

Overflow with hope, joy, and peace, by the power of my Holy Spirit!

Faithfully,
Your God of All Peace and Strength

BASED ON 1 PETER 1:3; EPHESIANS 1:18–19; AND ROMANS 15:13.

To teach is to learn.

CHINESE PROVERB

Let us not love with words or tongue but with actions and in truth.

1 JOHN 3:18

They do not love that do not show their love.

WILLIAM SHAKESPEARE

No one is useless in this world who lightens
the burden of it for anyone else.

CHARLES DICKENS

After the verb *to love,*
to help is the most beautiful verb in the world.

BARONESS BERTHA VON SUTTNER

We know that God's arithmetic is somewhat odd.
When you subtract by giving away, you get more.

ARCHBISHOP DESMOND TUTU

A child's life is like a piece of paper on which
every person leaves a mark.

CHINESE PROVERB

Anyone can count the seeds in an apple, but only God
can count the apples in a seed.

AUTHOR UNKNOWN

They won't care how much you know, until they know
how much you care.

AUTHOR UNKNOWN

*Now go; I will help you speak and
will teach you what to say.*

EXODUS 4:12

One joy scatters a hundred griefs.

CHINESE PROVERB

How great is the love the Father has lavished on us,
that we should be called children of God!
And that is what we are!

1 JOHN 3:1

THE PRAYER OF
ST. FRANCIS OF ASSISI

Lord, make me an instrument of your peace.
Where there is hatred, let me sow love.
Where there is injury, let me sow pardon.
Where there is doubt, let me sow faith.
Where there is despair, let me sow hope.
Where there is darkness, let me sow light.
Where there is sadness, let me sow joy. . . .

O Divine Master, grant that I may not so much
seek to be consoled, as to console;
to be understood, as to understand;
to be loved, as to love.
For it is in giving that we receive,
it is in pardoning that we are pardoned,
and it is in dying that we are born to eternal life.

"For I know the plans I have for you," declares the LORD,
"plans to prosper you and not to harm you,
plans to give you hope and a future."

JEREMIAH 29:11

True faith does not look at obstacles, but rather at God.

DONALD GREY BARNHOUSE

The LORD himself goes before you and will be with you;
he will never leave you nor forsake you. Do not be afraid;
do not be discouraged.

DEUTERONOMY 31:8

Dear One Who Guides My Children,

Teaching is no different than other parts of life in this world—filled with obstacles. But don't worry—I've already overcome everything you will face. I'll encourage your heart and strengthen you in every good deed and word. May you inspire and support one another daily. Be heart lifters, spurring one another on to love and good deeds.

Lovingly,
Your God of Nonstop Encouragement

BASED ON 2 THESSALONIANS 2:16–17;
1 THESSALONIANS 5:11; AND HEBREWS 10:24.

Each of us can be sure that
If God sends us on stony paths,
He will provide us with strong shoes,
And he will not send us out on any journey
For which he does not equip us well.

ALEXANDER MACLAREN

To learn, teach.

MASON COOLEY

*I will instruct you and teach you in the way you should go;
I will counsel you and watch over you.*

PSALM 32:8

If God leads you to it; he will lead you through it.

AUTHOR UNKNOWN

*But thanks be to God, who . . . through us spreads
everywhere the fragrance of the knowledge of him.*

2 CORINTHIANS 2:14

THE TWENTY-THIRD PSALM

The LORD is my shepherd,
I shall not be in want.
He makes me lie down in green pastures,
he leads me beside quiet waters,
he restores my soul.
He guides me in paths of righteousness
for his name's sake.

Even though I walk through the
valley of the shadow of death,
I will fear no evil, for you are with me;
Your rod and your staff, they comfort me.
You prepare a table before me in the
presence of my enemies.
You anoint my head with oil;
my cup overflows.
Surely goodness and love will follow
me all the days of my life,
and I will dwell in the house of the LORD forever.

I can do everything through [Christ]
who gives me strength.
PHILIPPIANS 4:13

TO THE ONE
WHO WAS LIFTED UP

Just as Moses lifted up the snake in the desert,
so the Son of Man must be lifted up,
that everyone who believes in him may have eternal life.
For God so loved the world that he gave his one and
only Son, that whoever believes in him shall not perish
but have eternal life.

JOHN 3:14–16

God has a thousand ways where I can see not one,
When all my means have reached their end,
Then his has just begun.

ESTHER GUYOT

The Son of Man did not come to be served,
but to serve, and to give his life as a ransom for many.

MATTHEW 20:28

The most important cross-reference
we can ever use is to reference the cross of Christ.

MONTE HAUN

*For no matter how many promises God has made,
they are "Yes" in Christ. And so through him the "Amen"
is spoken by us to the glory of God.
Now it is God who makes both us and you stand firm
in Christ. He anointed us, set his seal of
ownership on us, and put his Spirit in our hearts as a
deposit, guaranteeing what is to come.*

2 CORINTHIANS 1:20–22

Thou my everlasting portion,
More than friend or life to me;
All along my pilgrim journey,
Savior, let me walk with Thee.
Close to Thee, close to Thee;
Close to Thee, close to Thee;
All along my pilgrim journey,
Savior, let me walk with Thee.

FANNY J. CROSBY

*Come to me, all you who are weary and burdened,
and I will give you rest. Take my yoke upon you and learn
from me, for I am gentle and humble in heart, and you
will find rest for your souls. For my yoke is easy and
my burden is light.*

MATTHEW 11:28–30

Give us grace and strength to forbear and to persevere.

ROBERT LOUIS STEVENSON

*I have loved you with an everlasting love;
I have drawn you with loving-kindness.*

JEREMIAH 31:3

Dear One Who Teaches My Children,
I am the source of every good and perfect gift,
and I supply all your needs according to my endless
riches in glory. Be devoted to each other in brotherly
love, and teach with a servant heart, keeping Christ at
the center of all you do.

Graciously,
Your God of All Hope

BASED ON JAMES 1:17; PHILIPPIANS 4:19; ROMANS 12:10;
AND COLOSSIANS 3:17.

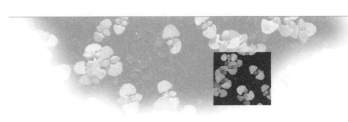

Attempt great things for God;
Expect great things from God.

WILLIAM CAREY

Therefore . . . stand firm. Let nothing move you. Always give yourselves fully to the work of the Lord, because you know that your labor in the Lord is not in vain.

1 CORINTHIANS 15:58

I have held many things in my hands,
and I have lost them all; but whatever I have placed in
God's hands, that I still possess.

AUTHOR UNKNOWN

He who dares to teach must always dare to learn.

ANONYMOUS

Those who hope in the LORD will renew their strength. They will soar on wings like eagles; they will run and not grow weary, they will walk and not be faint.

ISAIAH 40:31

If the Lord be with us, we have no cause of fear. His eye is upon us. His arm over us. His ear open to our prayer. His grace, sufficient. His promise, unchangeable.

JOHN NEWTON

AMAZING GRACE

Amazing grace! How sweet the sound
That saved a wretch like me!
I once was lost but now am found,
Was blind but now I see!

The Lord has promised good to me,
His Word my hope secures;
He will my shield and portion be
As long as life endures.

Through many dangers, toils, and snares
I have already come;
His grace has brought me safe so far,
His grace will see me home.

Yes, when this flesh and heart shall fail
And mortal life shall cease,
Amazing grace shall then prevail
In heaven's joy and peace.
JOHN NEWTON

Therefore, as God's chosen people, holy and dearly loved, clothe yourselves with compassion, kindness, humility, gentleness and patience. Bear with each other and forgive whatever grievances you may have against one another. Forgive as the Lord forgave you. And over all these virtues put on love, which binds them all together in perfect unity. Let the peace of Christ rule in your hearts. . . . And be thankful. . . . And whatever you do, whether in word or deed, do it all in the name of the Lord Jesus, giving thanks to God the Father through him.

COLOSSIANS 3:12–17

Even a small star shines in the darkness.

FINNISH PROVERB

Our gracious God not only leads us in the way of mercy, but he prepares our path before us, providing for all our wants even before they occur.

CHARLES SPURGEON

The LORD himself goes before you and will be with you; he will never leave you nor forsake you. Do not be afraid; do not be discouraged.

DEUTERONOMY 31:8

Things are getting out of hand . . . or maybe I'm discovering that things were never in my hands.

AUTHOR UNKNOWN

[Jesus said,] "You do not belong to the world,
but I have chosen you out of the world."

JOHN 15:19

SO THAT YOU
MIGHT LIFT CHRIST
UP TO OTHERS

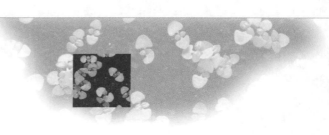

Trust in the LORD with all your heart and
lean not on your own understanding;
in all your ways acknowledge him,
and he will make your paths straight.

PROVERBS 3:5–6

A loving person lives in a loving world.
A hostile person lives in a hostile world.
Everyone you meet is your mirror.

KEN KEYES JR.

Dear One Who Comforts My Children,

I am he who comforts you! You have been chosen to bear my name. Teach my ways to your children. I will be your hiding place and will encourage you as I listen attentively to your requests. I will set your feet upon a rock and help you stand firmly.

Lovingly,
Your God of All Comfort

BASED ON ISAIAH 51:12; 1 SAMUEL 12:22; JEREMIAH 14:9;
DEUTERONOMY 6:7; PSALM 10:17; 32:7; AND 40:2.

Because you are made new through
Christ's cross and bear his name,
he himself empowers you to learn through
his Word and to teach others that . . .

. . . we are God's own. ....1 Samuel 12:22

He will never forsake us..Psalm 27:10

He crowns us with love and compassion..............Psalm 103:4

He loves us with an everlasting love......................Jeremiah 31:3

He sets us free ....John 8:36

We are his chosen ones...John 15:19

He delivers us ....Galatians 5:1

In his heart a man plans his course,
but the LORD determines his steps.

PROVERBS 16:9

Teachers touch eternity . . . one child at a time.

AUTHOR UNKNOWN

You will be a crown of splendor in the LORD'S hand, a royal
diadem in the hand of your God.

ISAIAH 62:3

Father, hear us, we are praying,
Hear the words our hearts are saying,
We are praying for our children.

Keep them from the powers of evil,
From the secret, hidden peril,
From the whirlpool that would suck them,
From the treacherous quicksand, pluck them.
From the worldling's hollow gladness,
From the sting of faithless sadness,
Holy Father, save our children.

Through life's troubled waters steer them,
Through life's bitter battle cheer them,
Father, Father, be Thou near them.
Read the language of our longing,
Read the wordless pleading thronging,
Holy Father, for our children.

And wherever they may bide,
Lead them home at eventide.

AMY CARMICHAEL
© 1999 The Dohnavur Fellowship

If faith can be seen every step of the way, it is not faith.

WILLIAM BARCLAY

We live by faith, not by sight.

2 CORINTHIANS 5:7

The closer we walk with God, the clearer
we see his guidance.

AUTHOR UNKNOWN

Dear One Who Encourages My Children,
Experience the constant feast of a cheerful heart as you
think about true and noble events. Reflect on memo-
ries that are lovely, pure, and right. Recall precious
moments that were honorable, extraordinary, and
praiseworthy! I will empower you to serve me faith-
fully with all your heart.

Faithfully,
Your Alpha and Omega

BASED ON PROVERBS 15:15; PHILIPPIANS 4:8;
AND 1 SAMUEL 12:24.

Those who walk with God always get
to their destination.

AUTHOR UNKNOWN

May our Lord Jesus Christ himself and God
our Father, who loved us and by his grace gave us eternal
encouragement and good hope, encourage your hearts
and strengthen you in every good deed and word.

2 THESSALONIANS 2:16–17

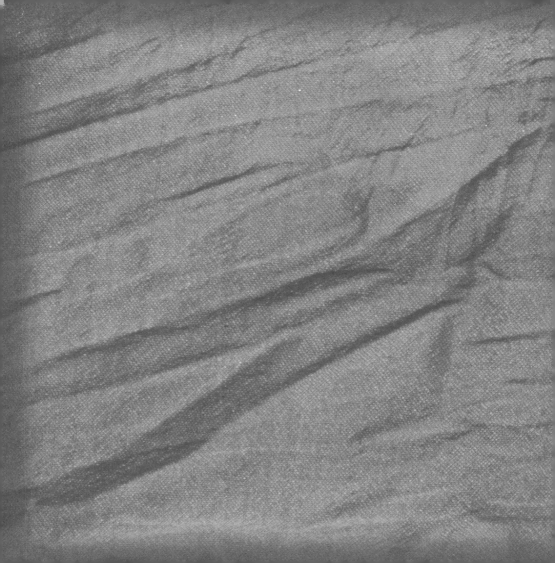